IMAGES OF ENGLAND

MUSWELL HILL
REVISITED

IMAGES OF ENGLAND

MUSWELL HILL
REVISITED

KEN GAY

TEMPUS

Frontispiece: The first St James's church, built in 1842 as shown in 1858. It was replaced by the present church in 1902.

First published 2006

Tempus Publishing Limited
The Mill, Brimscombe Port,
Stroud, Gloucestershire, GL5 2QG
www.tempus-publishing.com

© Ken Gay 2006

The right of Ken Gay to be identified as the Author
of this work has been asserted in accordance with the
Copyrights, Designs and Patents Act 1988.

British Library Cataloguing in Publication Data.
A catalogue record for this book is available from the British Library.

ISBN 0 7524 3835 2

Typesetting and origination by Tempus Publishing Limited.
Printed in Great Britain.

Contents

Acknowledgements

I am grateful to Deborah Hedgecock who suggested that I approach Tempus Publishing about producing another book on Muswell Hill, an idea developed whilst I was working as a volunteer on the image archive held at Bruce Castle. Deborah Hedgecock is the curator in charge of Bruce Castle Museum which houses Haringey's archives, formed from the collections previously held by the Boroughs of Tottenham, Wood Green and Hornsey. Many of the images in this book are from that archive, especially the more recent ones. The copyright of some of these has not been traced and I would be happy to have information about them.

I am also indebted to Hugh Garnsworthy and David Dell, two friends and fellow members of the Hornsey Historical Society who have both built up excellent collections of local images. They have both generously made their albums available to me without restraint. I must thank Joyce Horner for the wonderful 1912 wedding photograph and for the photograph of the Alexandra Palace Bowling Club dinner. I also thank Dr Elena Rowland for her photograph of
St James's school. Hornsey Historical Society archive has also helped. Aerofilms have allowed the use of the aerial photographs and English Heritage the photograph of the Uzielli almshouses. A number of images are my own.

Introduction

Muswell Hill takes its place name partly from a medieval holy well and partly from its location as a small settlement on top of a hill of that name. The mossy well had drawn pilgrims because, by repute, it had cured a Scottish king of a disease, a story recounted by the Tudor historian John Norden. The well was on farmland owned by nuns from London's Clerkenwell who were forced to demise their estate to the King's bottler after Henry VIII seized church lands in 1539.

From the sixteenth century onwards this hilly, forested area, located in the ancient parish of Hornsey in the county of Middlesex, gradually became more settled. Substantial houses with estate grounds were established, also farms, mainly dairy with hay as a valuable crop. Although estate occupiers were to include the Pulteney family, created Earls of Bath, and one estate was the summer residence of Topham Beauclerk, an aristocrat with royal antecedents, the residents were to become mainly Londoners who had made money as merchants, or professionals who wanted a rural retreat. They found it in this under-populated place of timbered beauty, set high and distant above the valleys of the Thames and the Lea.

A major local farm was purchased in 1863, along with The Grove estate next to it, to create Alexandra Park and to build on it a great Victorian exhibition and entertainment building, the Alexandra Palace. Opened in 1873, it was served by a branch line from Highgate, with a station at Muswell Hill. The village remained mostly unchanged after the railway came because local estate owners were not willing to sell off their ideal retreats and, indeed, one even bought an estate sold to a developer. In the 1880s land sold by the Palace Co. allowed some residential roads to be built but take up of houses was slow.

Muswell Hill survived as a rural place until 1896 even though Hornsey was rapidly built over, becoming a borough in 1903. But in 1896 James Edmondson bought a thirty-acre estate occupying flat land on the hilltop, laid out Queens and Princes Avenues across it and lined three sides with tall shopping parades. Thus he designed present-day Muswell Hill, with its concentrated inner core of shops forming a 'village' and its outlands covered with tree-lined avenues. An active local builder, W.J. Collins then added a residential estate over the former Fortismere and Firs estates, and after he bought the Avenue House estate two of his sons took over its development and created Rookfield Garden estate.

Muswell Hill has subsequently been lucky. Other districts were to see good older properties replaced by modern blocks but Muswell Hill's Edwardian buildings have escaped demolition. New buildings such as the 1936 Odeon or the blocks of flats in Colney Hatch Lane have replaced Victorian properties except for the unwelcome loss of the Athenaeum in Fortis Green Road. Other additions such as Summerlands Grange have fitted unobtrusively into the urban scene. Muswell Hill remains a good class residential suburb of family homes, just as when built, still enjoying untouched local woods and a nearby major park.

I have tried in this book to avoid using images I have already used in previous publications, especially my *Muswell Hill: History and Guide* and *Highgate & Muswell Hill* by Joan Schwitzer and myself, both published by Tempus. In my final chapters I have used images from the last decades of the twentieth century. As a local historian of some age I think that this period has now become part of our past. I am sure that the pictures of local shops will evoke memories in a way that Edwardian scenes, beyond personal experience, cannot achieve. Times move on and what was once contemporary has slipped away into becoming history.

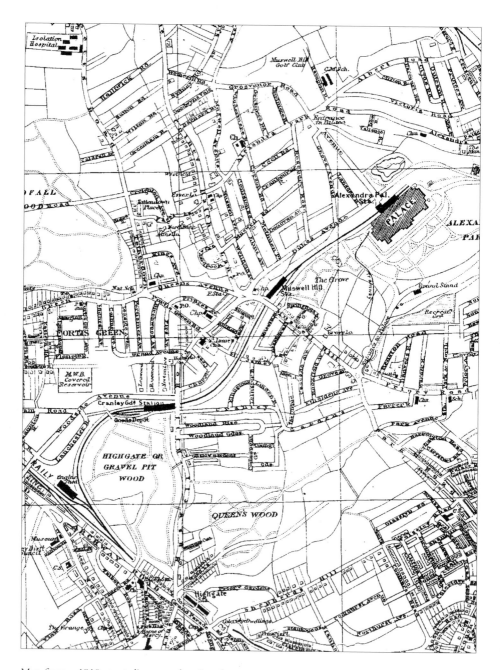

Map from a 1910 street directory showing the new avenues.

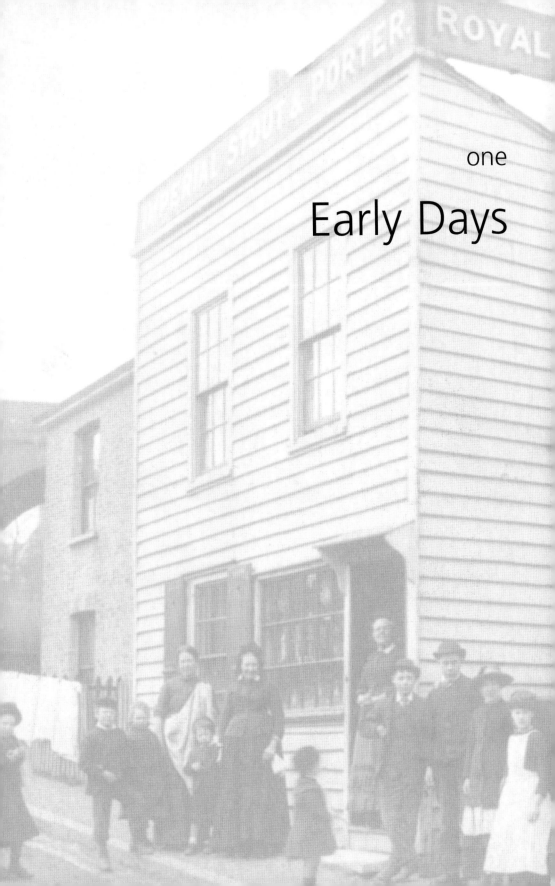

one

Early Days

Haymaking, photographed around 1880 at an unknown location at nearby Highgate. Hayricks were a common sight in the area, hay being in great demand as horse fodder, especially in London which was mainly dependent upon horses for transport. Arable farming had never been significant locally. Grasslands were used not only for hay but for grazing, mainly dairy cattle with some sheep.

Opposite above: The Green Man has stood at the top of Muswell Hill for centuries and is probably the ale house recorded for Muswell Hill in 1552. Photographed around 1880, the stone building stands next to a brick building which still survives and which probably dates from the late eighteenth century. It was formerly used as the village post office. Recently The Green Man has lost its old name.

Opposite below: The Royal Oak was situated at the lower end of St James's Lane from the eighteenth century, close to a small hamlet of cottages built next to Muswell Hill Common. The small weatherboarded building was finally replaced in 1966 by a larger pub of the same name.

Ladywood Cottages were among the old properties in St James's Lane. Council improvement schemes in the 1920s and 1930s saw the disappearance of the old cottages replaced by blocks of flats. A 1934 newspaper report said that some of the cottages were about 160 years old. This photograph was taken in 1935.

Friend's Cottages stood at the Muswell Hill end of Priory Road, at the entrance to Alexandra Park and racecourse. The people who lived there provided refreshments to visitors. This photograph dates from 1900.

Looking down Muswell Hill around 1900. Within a short while Avenue House estate (right), which stretched up the hill as far as St James's Lane, was built over when the Collins family developed the Rookfield Garden estate over its twenty-three acres. The Grove Lodge estate on the left still survives and its roadside lodge is still to be seen. The houses, far left, are late Victorian.

Brick cottages began to be built on the corner of Coppetts Road and Pages Lane from the 1860s, forming a tight square of properties. Many would have been occupied by artisans serving the needs of the mansions and villas of the area. The 1873 O.S. map labels them Tatterdown Place, the adjacent Tetherdown formerly being known as Tatterdown Lane.

The Grove was a twenty-four-acre estate near the top of Muswell Hill owned from 1837 by silk merchant William Block, probably the figure in this photograph taken around 1860. Block died in 1861 and the land was bought to help create Alexandra Park, opened in 1863, by a private

company. The mansion (far left) in a hollow near the road was demolished 1872. The Grove estate still remains as part of the now public park.

The Grove and Grove Lodge estates originated in a sixteenth-century property which separated into different ownerships. Grove Lodge, shown here, was a rebuild in 1854 of an earlier house by the owner George Attenborough, a jeweller. It was recently remodelled by Haringey Council, the current owners.

NORTH BANK. THE LAWN.

North Bank in Pages Lane also has surviving, largely unbuilt upon estate land. The house, dating from the 1860s, was the site of a nineteenth-century property known as The Hermitage. North Bank was bought in 1924 by Guy Chester and given to the Methodist church, and has remained since as a green lung for Muswell Hill.

This large recreational lake was in the grounds of Fortismere, an estate located between Fortis Green and Fortis Green Road. When frozen it was used for skating. The property and the adjacent Firs estate were bought by developer W.J. Collins around 1896. Collins lived temporarily in Fortismere Mansion but from 1902 laid out Grand Avenue and other roads to provide spacious residential housing. The lake was drained.

Colney Hatch Lane began to be lined from the 1840s with detached good-quality villas. Only three survive, Nos 3, 5 (shown) and 7. All on the west side of the road, they ran north past Pages Lane but most were replaced in the 1930s.

Muswell Hill Road, with still-surviving woodland each side, was once known as Southwood Lane and led towards Highgate village. On waste land bordering Churchyard Bottom Wood (now Queens Wood) a row of cottages were built as almshouses for the poor after manorial permission had been given by the Bishop of London in 1806. The cottages were demolished by 1898 when Queens Wood opened.

This footpath, photographed in 1884, is a continuation of Wood Lane and leads into Churchyard Bottom Wood, then owned by the Ecclesiastical Commissioners. In 1898 the woods were bought by Hornsey Council who renamed them Queens Wood in honour of Queen Victoria who had celebrated sixty years on the throne in 1897.

Cranley Dene at No. 152 Muswell Hill Road stood near the corner with Cranley Gardens and probably dated to the mid-nineteenth century. From 1912-1939 it housed Kings Head girls' school. By 1955 it was a home for the blind. Despite opposition locally, it was replaced in the 1980s by a brick-built block of residences for the elderly by Haringey Council.

Onslow Gardens was already partly built up by 1896. This turning off Muswell Hill Road, just north of Queens Wood, was intended to be part of a residential estate called Imperial Park, planned by the Imperial Property Investment Co. Nearby Cranley Gardens was devised as part of the scheme; the proposed development followed the 1885 purchase by the company of forty-two-acre Upton Farm. The farmhouse stood in Muswell Hill Road where Cranley Gardens now is.

Woodlands was a seven-acre estate with a mansion standing between Upton Farm and Queens Wood dating from the mid-nineteenth century. From 1861 until 1875 it was the Lehmann family country home where they entertained the leading literary and art figures of the day. Here Wilkie Collins wrote his novel *Man and Wife*. This photograph of the rear was taken just before demolition in 1890.

Woodlands Rise and Woodlands Gardens were built over the grounds by a Mr R. Metherall who developed the land.

Woodlands stables with a clock tower stood on the opposite side of Muswell Hill Road and was also photographed in 1890 before demolition. The strip of land also contained a gardener's cottage and kitchen gardens.

The strip was used between 1902-04 as the site of a tall block containing apartments and ground-level shops named Cranley Mansions and Parade. This building still stands. The branch line to Alexandra Palace crossed Muswell Hill Road a little to the north and in 1902 Cranley Gardens station was opened on the same side of the road. This survived only to the 1960s.

Almshouses for five poor persons were provided in 1861 by a Madame Uzielli. They were built in Pages Lane on a site near North Bank and were subsequently known as Uzielli Cottages.

They survived until the 1930s but by 1938 Whitehall Lodge, a modernist block of flats, had been built on their site.

This stone pillar is between the former grounds of the Uzielli almshouses and the adjacent school and may be a surviving boundary marker for the almshouses, being in the same Gothic style. The almshouses once abutted the grounds of Springfield House; in 1907 this was taken by French nuns for a convent who then built a girls' school onto Springfield House. It subsequently became a Roman Catholic primary school.

Pages Lane was a back lane connecting Colney Hatch Lane with Tetherdown and the former Hornsey common. It has previously been known as Red House Lane and Jones Lane. Before development it was much narrower, as this photograph shows.

Pages Lane at the junction with Creighton Avenue which was laid out by 1900. Still recognisable is the White House (right) but the tree has long gone. A modern mini-roundabout now occupies its site.

St James photographed in 1896. A church council meeting that year considered its future and decided, with advice from two architects, to replace it as it was in bad repair. It was pulled down in 1900 and the present St James built in its place. The Victorian pillar box on the corner of St James's Lane survives.

In the foreground is the site of the historic well which gave Muswell Hill its name. In 1900 builder C.W. Scott erected houses here and 'removed the pump to my own house as a historic relic'. A plaque placed on No. 40 Muswell Road in the late 1940s marks where the well was. Alexandra Palace, in the background, was just coming into local authority ownership in 1900.

Above: Muswell Road was laid out by 1885 over land belonging to the Alexandra Park Co. and sold off for housing with parliamentary permission. The road follows the line of the track to the well. The upper part of the road nearest Colney Hatch Lane has Victorian houses, although take up of them was slow before the Edwardian suburb was built.

Right: Hillside, one of the Victorian houses in Muswell Road, was once the home of John Samuel Alder (1847-1919), the architect who designed the present St James church. He designed several other local churches for the London Diocese, including the church and vicarage for St Andrews in Alexandra Park Road where he was to be a sidesman. Its foundation stone was laid in 1903.

The Weslyan Methodist church on the corner of Colney Hatch Lane with Alexandra Park Road was designed by a Methodist architect, Josiah Gunton. The adjacent building, designed by architect Arthur Boney, was used for the Sunday school. The church dated from 1899 and the other building soon after. Both were demolished in 1984.

Hornsey Isolation Hospital was erected in 1889 by Hornsey Local Board on former waste land at the northern end of Coppetts Road. It was for the reception of persons suffering from infectious diseases, and it was expanded and became a joint hospital with Wood Green and Finchley in the 1920s. From 1968 it was an integral part of the Royal Free Hospital. In recent years its land has been sold for housing, but it still operates.

two

Alexandra Park and Palace

Alexandra Park opened in July 1863 as a commercial speculation with the Palace under construction by 1866. The banqueting hall of 1864 was the first building and was used for various purposes including an indoor rifle range. In the 1920s it was converted into a ballroom, with a maple dance floor and the capacity for 1,000 dancers. During the 1940s it was a wartime clothing factory and became known as Blandford Hall after the firm using it. It mysteriously burnt down in 1971.

The racecourse in the foreground was opened in June 1868, five years before the opening of the first Palace in 1873. With a grandstand and paddocks it occupied some forty acres of flat land. The course was closed by the Jockey Club in 1970 and in time the course was reabsorbed into the park. The first Palace burnt down soon after its opening. In this view it is the second Palace, opened in 1875, which dominates the landscape.

Before the Palace opened in 1873 a branch railway was built connecting the building by rail with Highgate and thence to Kings Cross. Combined rail and admission tickets were issued. Although the branch line has long gone, still standing is the massive seventeen-arch viaduct taking it across St James's Lane. The arches are used for workshops.

Steam trains were deployed on the branch line which was operated by the Great Northern Railway Co. until in 1923 it became part of the London North Eastern Railway (LNER). The trains carried not only local commuters, visitors to the Palace and freight but also coal to heat the Palace building. Passenger services ceased in July 1954.

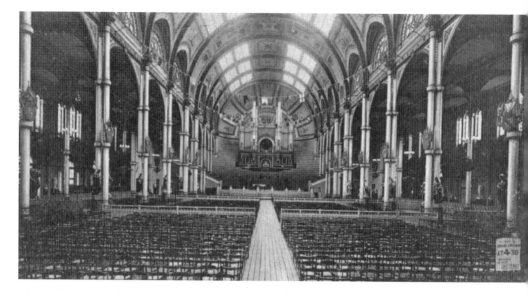

Above: The Great Hall was the central feature of the 1875 Palace, 386ft long and 184ft wide, seating 12,000 people. The organ built by Henry Willis outstripped others in the country in size, design and equipment. It was driven by two basement steam engines. Circuses, flower shows and exhibitions were staged here.

Large, glass-roofed conservatories were built at both the east and west ends of the 1875 Palace. Tropical plants were grown. Glass folding doors formed the partition walls of hall, conservatories and corridors, allowing the entire centre of the building to open out.

CONSERVATORY ALEXANDRA PALACE.

Above: The conservatory at the west end is known today as the Palm Court. The one at the east end is now the foyer to the 1988 ice rink. The glass roofs echo great Victorian glass house constructions at Kew and Chatsworth from where Paxton conceived the idea of the 1851 exhibition halls in Hyde Park known as the Crystal Palace.

Opposite below: The orchestra stalls around the organ could seat an additional 2,000 people. Choristers and large groups of musicians would render great choral works. The Alexandra Palace Choir and Orchestra numbered over 600 in Edwardian times. Handel's *Messiah* was often performed on Good Fridays. American composer Sousa and his band often visited to play.

Above: An aviary helped display the collection of birds built up by the trustees, often gifts from the public. Today it is common to cage budgerigars, canaries, parrots and pigeons but in earlier days wild birds such as sparrows, linnets and chaffinches (given to the Palace by a local inhabitant) were kept but were said to be well looked after.

Above: From the beginning the 'Palace of the People' was described as being at Muswell Hill. This was in the ancient parish of Hornsey and its boundary with the neighbouring ancient parish of Tottenham ran across the park, though in 1888 the area was part of a new local authority for Wood Green, separated from Tottenham. In June 1893 the custom of beating the boundaries brought this group into the park.

Right: The Palace was a Victorian concept and typically big in size. Maintenance of the vast fabric and the park, heating of the building and labour costs meant a constant struggle to obtain sufficient income from visitors to keep it going. Its Victorian origins are symbolised by column decorations restored after the 1980 fire.

Opposite below: Small animals were also given and kept, including monkeys and a bear called Nelson. At one time birds and animals were under the care of a Captain Henry, a former lion tamer. There were also cases of stuffed animals. In 1905 admission was 1*d.*

Left: A commercial failure, a group of local authorities including Middlesex County Council bought the Palace and park (but not all the estate) to save the open space from the builders of the advancing suburbs. Attendances were boosted by electric tram services to each end of the building, overcoming the steep, off-putting gradients.

Below: From December 1905 single-decker trams ran from Turnpike Lane to the west end of the Palace and from February 1906 double-decker trams ran along Priory Road to the foot of Muswell Hill by the entrance to the park where they terminated. From April 1906 trams also ran from Wood Green to the east end of the Palace.

Opposite below: The trams were installed just too late to bring visitors to see another possible transport miracle, a pioneering airship. Constructed by Dr Barton in a shed east of the Palace and paid for by the trustees, it brought nearly 15,000 people to see it at a fee of 3*d* each. Due to have War Office trials (Germany was developing the Zeppelin), it was launched in July 1905 but was damaged after landing in Essex and the project was dropped.

ALEXANDRA PARK 1906

Above: One of the single-decker trams which ran up to the Palace. The steepness of the hill prevented the Metropolitan Electric Tramway Co. from using double-deckers. Light street railways began in America from 1888 and were to be installed by local authorities in the UK, the first in London starting in 1901. Existing horse tram routes were electrified and new lines laid down, and were seen, rather than omnibuses, as the best way of obtaining less congested streets.

Under local authority ownership the Palace hosted many events and the park proved a popular local amenity for the region. A wide range of activities took place including balloon ascents and parachute descents, rallies, group visits by children and firework displays.

The boating lake attracted visitors who hired boats, fished or just watched the wildfowl. It was the setting for some spectacular evening firework events, with dramatised scenes.

The Grove area, the remnant of the old landed estate, was noted for its general beauty and was the setting for Sunday concerts and even outdoor dancing. The main avenue of trees is known as Dr Johnson's Walk, commemorating the visits here by the great eighteenth-century dictionary maker and literary giant during the tenancy of the estate by Topham Beauclerk.

The Grove changes in appearance as the trees are managed but has always appealed as a special haven where nature might be enjoyed. It also had a convenient tearoom and a bandstand on the upper slope.

In the spring of 1902 some 2,500 colonial troops attending the Coronation of King Edward VII were quartered in Alexandra Park using tents. The Coronation was deferred till August 1902, due to the King's illness. Here the south slope is used for an inspection by Field Marshall Roberts, C-in-C of the British Army.

The officers camp in Alexandra Park including a turbaned officer. As the King's Consort was now Queen Alexandra, the choice of Alexandra Park for the colonial troops was perhaps appropriate.

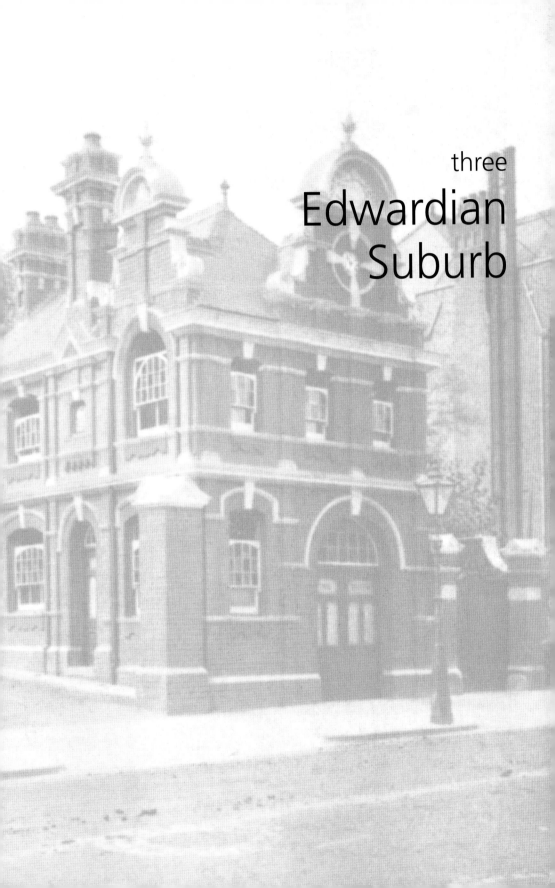

three

Edwardian
Suburb

This 1897 date stone records the birth of the new suburb. It can be seen in Princes Avenue above a door at the end of Queens Parade which was the first of the shopping parades built by Edmondson after he acquired the land in 1896. Edmondson created the shopping centre and surrounded it with residential avenues.

Muswell Hill railway station on the Hill opened in 1873 on the new line to Alexandra Palace. Little housing development followed, the 1894 O.S. map showing Muswell Hill still dominated by country estates. These were occupied by wealthy London merchants or professionals. Change began in 1896, on a large scale.

Edmondson was able to build a shopping centre each side of Muswell Hill Road (since 1960 called Muswell Hill Broadway) as, after his purchase of The Limes and Fortis House estate, other landowners sold their properties here and in Colney Hatch Lane to him. In this Edwardian view Princes Parade is on the left and Victoria Parade on the former Hillfield Park estate on the right.

Queens Parade (left) faces a villa which survived until 1927 when it was replaced by Lloyds Bank. That side of the road was in fragmented ownership. Further on, however, was the Summerlands estate on which developer Thomas Finnane built Summerlands Parade and Mansions from 1904, a matching parade.

This photograph of the roundabout was taken before it became a bus terminus in 1902, but after Queens Parade was built in 1897. The Presbyterian church (now a pub) which has a 1902 foundation stone is not to be seen beyond Queens Parade (right). The view catches the newly built suburb at its beginnings.

Queens Avenue was the first residential road devised by Edmondson and intended to be its finest. It was made 65ft wide, unusual at that time, especially as there was no motorised traffic to speak of in 1897. Properties are terraced but substantial in size; some are now hotels.

This brick fire station was erected in Queens Avenue in 1899 on a site donated by Edmondson, near the roundabout. When a modern station was built in Fortis Green in 1926 the building became redundant and was used as a council depot until Muswell Hill public library was built on its site in 1931. A service road runs down its side, provided at the back of all parades by Edmondson, though often as cul-de-sacs.

Dukes Avenue was laid out by Edmondson over the former eleven-acre Elms estate after he bought it in 1899. The site of the old mansion was given by him to the Baptists for a church, built in 1902. The Exchange shopping parades facing the roundabout were built by him.

The Wellfield estate, east of Colney Hatch Lane, abutted the estate and Edmondson bought this at the same time from the same owner. This enabled him to run avenues from Dukes Avenue to Muswell Road. The first of these was Wellfield Avenue.

The next residential road was Elms Avenue. These parallel avenues contain some of Edmondson's finest properties, built when Edwardian domestic architecture was at its best, using an Arts and Crafts freestyle, mixing Baroque with vernacular detailing. Importantly, the suburb was built homogenously in the same style.

Above: Methuen Park, named after a Boer War commander, was the next avenue turning off Dukes Avenue. The Edmondson sales board advertises electric light which was then beginning to displace gas lighting. Domestic electricity supply was to transform households.

Overleaf: Horse-drawn buses began to serve the suburb from 1901 regularly. This photograph from around 1912 shows the magnificent two-horse vehicles. They were about to be replaced by petrol buses. Horses continued to be used to draw delivery carts until well into the 1960s, latterly mainly for milk and coal.

The horse buses needed a terminus, or 'stand', and this was provided from 1902 at the roundabout. This continued to be used after conversion to petrol buses, gradually taking up a larger space. In 1904 a busmen's shelter was provided by local donations. The present building on the roundabout dates from 1926.

Bus route No. 111 between Muswell Hill and Finsbury Park via Crouch End (now the No. W7 route) began operating in 1914. It severely reduced the number of passengers using the railway for this journey.

Right: Road surfaces were earth or gravel before tarmac began to be used from 1910. Setts enabled pedestrians to cross from one pavement to the next cleanly to avoid mud and horse droppings. This one is in Woodberry Crescent (north arm) parallel to Colney Hatch Lane.

Below: In addition foot scrapers enabled mud to be knocked off footwear before entering a building. This one survives opposite the roundabout outside a former bank, now the Giraffe Restaurant.

By 1901 the population had risen locally from under 2,000 to nearly 6,000. The railway station down the hill (centre) began to be well used. On the right is the old White House building with the pillars of the Express Dairy next to it.

The Express Dairy acquired Belle Vue Lodge and opened a milk depot and adjacent tea room, elegantly dated AD 1900. Taken before its 1980s closure, this photograph shows its size. Founder George Barham chose the company's name to symbolise his pioneering transport of milk by express train in special churns he designed.

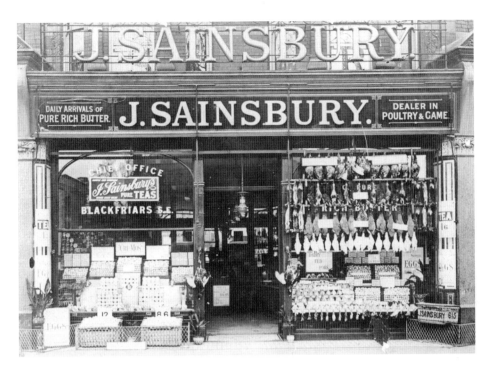

J. Sainsbury opened its Muswell Hill branch at No. 4 The Exchange in 1901. The Exchange parades facing the roundabout had been built by Edmondson at that time. Sainsbury operated at these premises until 1966 when they moved into supermarket premises in Fortis Green Road. Their former shop is currently Pizza Express.

Pulham & Sons, the butchers at No. 16 Victoria Parade, was a much appreciated local shop which was to survive until the 1980s. This magnificent Christmas display probably dates from 1910.

Left: This newsagents near the top of Dukes Avenue still bears the Cummins name. W.R. Cummins began as a newspaper boy but established shops here and in Colney Hatch Lane selling papers and stationery. He founded *The Muswell Hill Record* in 1907 with a printing press by 1915. He also ran nurseries and sold flowers.

Below: Langton's clock is still a feature of the Broadway although not functional, and Langton's the jewellers has long gone. Special clock mechanisms were to be seen inside. This photograph of its installation, taken around 1905, shows that wireless apparatus allowed the clock to receive Greenwich Mean Time and other signals.

Special WIRELESS Apparatus is now installed for receiving GREENWICH MEANTIME and other SIGNALS.

Opposite above: Rowley & Louis traded in Summerland Gardens and were still there in 1939. This photograph, dating from around 1914, show an early motor trade business. The first petrol-driven vehicles appeared on British roads in the late nineteenth century. The first recorded use of the word 'garage' is in 1902 (OED). Early planning applications called them 'motor sheds'.

Opposite below: Muswell Hill expanded south along Muswell Hill Road towards the Highgate Woods, with W.J. Collins among the house builders. The increased population here encouraged the opening in 1902 of Cranley Gardens station on the branch line from the Palace. Collins was the second major developer, building properties in similar style to Edmondson.

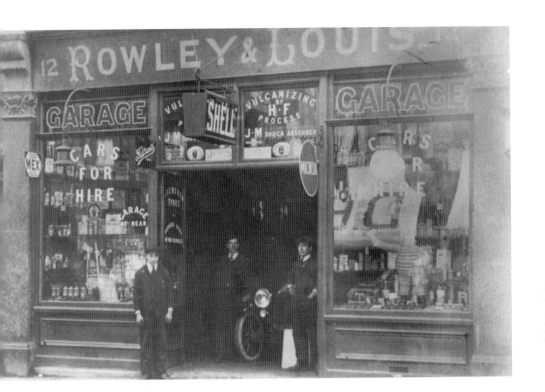

Creighton Avenue was cut through Coldfall Woods in 1901 and curved round to join Pages Lane at its eastern end. This exceptional view shows the first houses at this end, with the Weslyan church and Essex Lodge in the distance in Colney Hatch Lane.

Edmondson extended Princes Parade (right) into Fortis Green Road and built the Athenaeum next to it. It was given as a community centre. He built St James's Parade beyond it in 1901.

Athenaeum,-View of Proscenium, Muswell Hill.
E 19710

The Athenaeum had a large and a small hall and was used for drama and music and from 1920 as a silent cinema. It accommodated a girls' school and was the venue for a debating society called Muswell Hill Parliament. It housed a spiritualist church and a synagogue. It was demolished in 1966 and replaced by flats with Sainsbury at ground level.

St James's Parade still bears its old name (no longer its postal address) and its 1901 date stone. The turreted corner by the tree was bombed in the Second World War and the site was used from 1959 by The John Baird pub.

This cedar tree stood on the lawn in front of Fortis House. When Princes Avenue was laid out and Fortis Green Road widened, requests were made for it to be kept. Edmondson saved the tree and gave the corner site to the public for ever. The tree survived until 1918 but other trees were then planted as replacements.

In 2006 the barber shop opposite the corner garden celebrated 100 years of hairdressing on the site. The shop is at the end of Firs Parade built by W.J. Collins on the perimeter of his Firs and Fortismere estates which he purchased in 1896 and then developed with residential avenues matching those of Edmondson on the other side of Fortis Green Road.

Firs Avenue runs down to Grand Avenue which is connected by four others laid out by W.J. Collins over the former Firs and Fortismere estates, most of them leasehold. They were built as good terraced family houses, but without garages from 1902.

TETHERDOWN MUSWELL HILL.

Tollington Boys school (left) was opened in 1902. It was built by William Campbell Brown in the front garden of his Tetherdown villa called Thorntons which was later joined to it. It was a branch of a school established by his father in Stroud Green, hence its name. It successfully provided a private school for the suburb.

An off-shoot of Tollington catering for girls opened in 1908 in a nearby Tetherdown villa opposite the later-built Kings Avenue. The building has been used for various educational purposes after the girls moved out.

In 1911 Tollington girls moved into a purpose-built building at the junction of Grand Avenue and Collingwood Avenue, and operated, like the boys, as a grammar school, both being taken over by Middlesex County Council. In 1958 the girls moved in with the boys into a new block in Tetherdown which eventually became Fortismere Comprehensive. This building became Tetherdown Primary school.

Fourteen women, mostly in white Edwardian dresses, pose for a photograph of the S.J.S. Cricket Team, Muswell Hill. The cross on the shield confirms that this was probably attached to St James's church. They may have played either at Alexandra Park or at Crouch End playing fields.

Golf was another sport engaged in by Edwardian women. By 1905 there were 100 members of the Muswell Hill Golf Club which had been established in 1893 on land owned by the Alexandra Palace Co. north of the Palace. By 1900 it had moved had to its present site and used the farmhouse of former Tottenham Wood farm as a club house. They moved into a new club house in 1931 and only the portico remains of the old farmhouse.

Alexandra Park Road was laid out by 1889 and connected Colney Hatch Lane with Wood Green.
It was soon to accommodate two Anglican churches both designed by J.S. Alder, architect of St James.
St Andrews dated from 1903 and St Saviour's from 1904, both serving the newly developed estates built
over land formerly belonging to company owning Alexandra Palace and Park. St Saviour was demolished
in 1994 when the congregation transferred to St Andrews.

Rosebery Road connects Dukes Avenue with Alexandra Park Road and was entirely built by Charles
Rook, a prolific local developer. There is a 1907 date stone on the shop corner where it joins Alexandra
Park Road. Earl Rosebery was prime minister from 1894-96 and won the Derby in 1894, 1895 and
1905; Alexandra Park racecourse was nearby.

Curzon Road connects Alexandra Park Road with Muswell Road and is named after Lord Curzon who was Viceroy of India from 1899-1906. This Edwardian photograph shows the young trees which Hornsey council planted along the new suburban avenues.

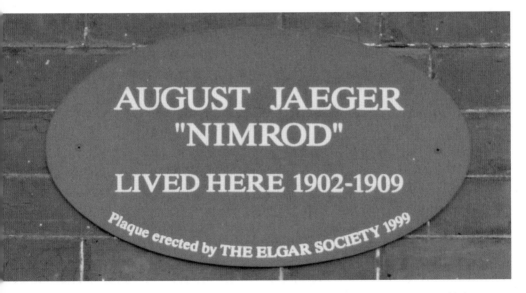

No. 37 Curzon Road was the home from 1902-09 of August Jaegar. The German music publisher was a friend of Edward Elgar who visited here. Elgar named one of his *Enigma Variations* 'Nimrod' after his friend as Jaeger means Hunter, and Nimrod was a hunter. The plaque was erected in 1999 by The Elgar Society at the urging of music critic Felix Aprahamian, who lived nearby in Methuen Park.

This impressive wedding photograph dates from June 1912 and was taken in the back garden of No. 116 Dukes Avenue. The bridegroom is Frank Horner and the bride is Maud Bailey whose parents had lived in the house since 1906. The marriage took place at the Weslyan Methodist church and was to

last sixty years. Frank Horner's shipping work took him from the twenty years between the two world wars, to South Africa. Maud's parents lived at No. 116 until 1946, narrowly missing a wartime bomb outside No. 110 which failed to explode.

Between 1906 and 1910 Edmondson built over the North Lodge estate creating Woodberry Crescent (named after his own house). He fronted Colney Hatch Lane with a residential terrace of houses which he named Sunnyside, probably because they faced east.

Springfield Avenue had been laid out parallel to Muswell Hill on land formerly the site of The Grove mansion and estate. It was built up in this Edwardian period by fine houses and maisonettes in Arts and Crafts style by the Collins family.

Across the road on the former Avenue House estate which the Collins family had bought in December 1899, Rookfield Garden estate was laid out, taking its name from Rookfield, a mansion on the Avenue House estate. It followed contemporary Garden City principles, with low housing density, irregular groupings of houses built in vernacular styles and green spaces. Nos 19 and 21 Rookfield Avenue had been the site of Avenue House.

Cascade Avenue on the Rookfield estate probably derives its name from St James's Brook, a tributary of the Moselle Brook which crossed the land and formed lakes on it. Natural watercourses have long been culverted underground.

In 1903, on the north side of Fortis Green, near Tetherdown, a Hornsey council depot was established. Designed to assist highway work it had stabling for seven horses and provided sheds for stores, a men's rest room and a horsekeeper's cottage (centre). The depot site was sold around 2000 and used for housing.

Fortis Green branch fire station was adjacent to the depot. The more substantial brick building pictured was provided in 1926. In 1963 a new fire station opened in Priory Road, Hornsey and this site was then used for a clinic.

In 1907 W.J. Collins built Leaside Mansions opposite the fire station and paid tribute to the firemen by including decorative shields over the doorways which had firemen's helmets and axes.

Eight firemen's cottages were built behind the fire station and these still survive and are occupied. Two extra houses were built on the site recently.

Fortis Green Brewery once stood further along Fortis Green, adjacent to the Clissold Arms pub.
Probably dating from the early nineteenth century and brewing ale for travellers on the Great North
Road at East Finchley it was from the 1880s operated by Norman & Co. It was then taken over by Ind.
Coope & Co. The site was redeveloped from 1903.

Above: The Clissold Arms has become famous as the debut venue of The Kinks in 1957, a pop band formed by Ray Davies who lived opposite in Denmark Terrace. It is probably early nineteenth century. The name may derive from Augustus Clissold after whom Clissold Park in Stoke Newington is named. He married a wealthy heiress and gave his name to their estate.

Right: Demolition of the brewery freed a site for a police station for Muswell Hill, built on the corner with Fortis Green Avenue. The sturdy building with its 1904 date stone was provided with stabling at the rear for six horses. Its future is uncertain.

The Alexandra, another nineteenth-century pub, stood on the other side of Fortis Green from the Clissold Arms. It was named after the Danish Princess Alexandra who came to England in 1863 to marry the Prince of Wales, the future King Edward VII. Denmark Terrace is nearby, and Alexandra Park, opened in 1863, is named after her.

The Alexandra, which still operates, acquired a 1930s roadhouse style exterior in the inter-war years. Fortunately it has retained its historic name, unlike other public houses.

four

Between
the Wars

AND AVENUE, N.

Left: This elegant, tucked-away building is St James's Vicarage and nestles behind the church in St James's Lane. Its foundation stone was laid in 1915 on the site of the former parsonage.

Below: Fortis Court was built 1926 by W.B. Collins on the corner of Fortis Green Road and Fortis Green. The site was once the driveway into Fortismere, the old mansion. Woodside Mansions opposite, on the corner with Tetherdown, was also built by Billy Collins at this time. Both are good brick buildings, perhaps influenced in style by the architect Edwin Lutyens.

Opposite below: Dorchester Court in Colney Hatch Lane, on the corner of Muswell Road, was another tall block of flats to arrive in Muswell Hill in the 1930s, despite resistance to flats from Hornsey councillors. Built further north in Colney Hatch Lane in the 1930s were Barrington Court, Cedar Court, St Ivian Court and Seymour Court.

Above: On the north side of Fortis Green, Collins later built Long Ridges in 1930 and Twyford Court, illustrated, in 1931. Coldfall Wood which had once reached Fortis Green had been cut back, allowing the Coldfall estate to be built to the north in 1924-26.

Tetherdown Hall was built in 1928-29 opposite the Congregational church and was designed by architect Stanley Griffiths who was a member of the church. This photograph was taken in 1963.

Tetherdown in the 1930s gained this terrace of houses, built on the site of former greenhouses. The curved bays with Crittall metal windows were typical of the period. No. 72 was the first house bought by actor Peter Sellars. This photograph dates from 1964.

Tollington in Tetherdown flourished as a grammar school for Muswell Hill between the wars, controlled by Middlesex County Council. This view of the rear was taken in 1927.

Tollington school opened this swimming pool on site in 1933 after several years of fund-raising. It gave decades of service but currently is drained and out of use on what is now the Fortismere school site.

Above: In 1931 a major gain for Muswell Hill was a public library in Queens Avenue. This obviated the need to travel to either Highgate or Tottenham Lane, Hornsey to borrow books or look in a newspaper for an advertised job. It was designed by W.H. Adams, Hornsey's borough surveyor in consultation with the borough librarian.

Above: Constructed between 1928-30 this neat neo-Georgian block is the administrative headquarters for St Luke's Hospital for the mentally ill. In 1927 the hospital had acquired three Victorian mansions in Woodside Avenue, close to Highgate Woods. The thirty-acre site was used to build not only this block but wards in the grounds. An exit into Grand Avenue was also made.

Right: Our Lady of Muswell Roman Catholic church was built on the site of No. 1 Colney Hatch Lane, a villa named Oncot acquired in 1917. Its foundation stone was laid in 1938 and it came into use in 1939. Seating 600 the architect was T.H.B. Scott. Consecration was in 1959.

Opposite below: Valette Court and adjacent residential flats were built by Hornsey in St James's Lane in 1934. They replaced old cottages deemed not up to health standards. It is named after Cllr L.J. Valette who was to become mayor in 1946-47.

Above: The Odeon opened in September 1936, part of a complex built on the corner of Muswell Hill and Fortis Green Roads comprising cinema, shops and flats. It is the only Odeon to retain its view from the balcony intact. This photograph shows its dramatic linear light fittings and Streamline Art Deco style. Listed Grade II starred by English Heritage, the cinema has never closed in its seventy-year history.

Right: During the inter-war years concerts continued to be held in The Grove in Alexandra Park. This 1924 programme advertises a concert party. The brochure also advertises dancing in the ballroom from 7.30–11 p.m. every Thursday and Saturday. This was in the former banqueting hall in the park.

Below: In this 1934 photograph the Salvation Army Wood Green Citadel Band stand in their impressive uniforms in front of the Palace's south front. These steps were repositioned after the 1980s fire.

Opposite below: The Ritz cinema at the top of Muswell Hill opened three months after the Odeon and from 1962 was to be operated by the ABC chain. A stylish building, it nevertheless closed in 1978, when television had reduced cinema audiences, and was demolished in 1980 to be replaced by a tall brick office block.

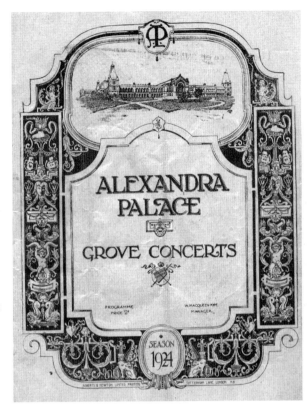

ALEXANDRA PALACE

GROVE CONCERTS

PROGRAMME PRICE 2D.

W. MACQUEEN-POPE MANAGER.

SEASON 1924

The Alexandra Palace Bowling Club annual dinner, probably in 1935, showing a high standard of formal dress. Play was on an outside rink near the east end of the Palace. There was also an Alexandra Palace

Indoor Bowls Club from October 1909, playing on two coconut matting rinks. This Indoor Club survived until the 1990s. The outside rink fell into disuse and was removed in the 1980s.

ALEXANDRA PALACE

Secretary - W. Warren Dingle

EASTER MONDAY

Programme & Time Table

WITH PLAN OF THE PALACE

LOOK FOR THE RED STAR

Turn to the Centre Page and if a RED STAR
is stamped in the space provided you will be
admitted **FREE** to Skating Rink or Ballroom

April 2, 1934   **PRICE TWOPENCE**

THE ALEXANDRA PALACE OPERATIC AND DRAMATIC SOCIETY
"A COUNTRY GIRL"

Above left: The Easter Monday Programme at the Palace in 1934 offered free admission to the Skating
Rink or Ballroom if a red star was stamped inside. The view of the south front shows a dearth of trees
and vegetation, just lawns and paths. In the following year the BBC would take over the east tower and
erect its mast on it, ready for television transmissions.

Above right: The Alexandra Palace Amateur Operatic & Dramatic Society was formed in 1924. *The
Country Girl* was one of its productions. In 1922 the theatre had been restored by theatre professional
W. MacQueen Pope who lived in nearby Etheldene Avenue and who was the Palace Manager from 1922
to 1924.

Right: The mast erected by the BBC in 1935 ready for television transmissions to domestic receivers in November 1936 became a familiar symbol because it fronted the twice-weekly new film which they were to broadcast. The mast was 215ft high. The tower was given bay windows.

Below: The Coronation of King George VI in May 1937 was celebrated across the country, often with street tea parties. Here Coldfall Wood school children parade in a turning off Grand Avenue, Muswell Hill. The Coronation procession was the first outside broadcast of television made by a mobile BBC television unit. The ceremony was covered mainly by radio; fifty-eight microphones were used during the day, with thirty-two installed in Westminster Abbey.

Left: Grand Avenue on 11 May 1941, after an air raid. Blast has shattered windows and shifted roof tiles. On 19 April St James's church had been gutted. Bombs fell in Collingwood Avenue, between Leaside and Fortismere Avenues and in Firs Avenue in this area alone.

Below: A V2 rocket fell towards the end of the war at the top of Muswell Hill, damaging the branch line to the Palace and properties behind the Ritz cinema car park.

five

Peace Again

Muswell Hill seen from the air is a low rise suburb, St James's church standing tall not far from the bulk of the Odeon, with the 1928 telephone exchange prominent in Grand Avenue in the

foreground. The auditorium of the Ritz cinema looms over the post-war Summerland Grange blocks, with Alexandra Park beyond.

Love blossomed even in winter in the quiet stretches of Highgate Woods, pictured here in December 1960. Muswell Hill's immediate surroundings provided a ring of foliage, with not only Highgate and Queens Woods, Coldfall Wood, Alexandra Park and Crouch End Playing Fields, but also the green path of the Parkland Walk from 1984.

Post-war there was a need for more homes. In 1949 a field adjacent to Alexandra Park was used by Hornsey Council to make a 'dog-leg' extension to existing Springfield Avenue and for a cul-de-sac of 1950s houses to be built. The Palace is in the background (left), half hidden by posts.

This maternity home in Alexandra Park Road on a corner with Muswell Avenue was convenient for the post-war baby boom. It had been there since at least the 1920s and when photographed here in 1960 was a well-used local facility. It was replaced in the 1980s by senior citizen residences, babies grown old.

Babies grow up and go to primary school. This 1952 photograph is of St James's school in Fortis Green. The seated man (right) is headmaster Mr I.T. Plant who had just published the school's history and who was soon to retire. To the right of him in the photograph is deputy head Mrs Frances Lewis. Opened by the church in 1850 this was the first school ever in Muswell Hill. It is now in Woodside Avenue.

Opposite below: Post-war youth was catered for by Chester House, built by the Methodist church between 1959 and 1960 on the corner of Pages Lane and Colney Hatch Lane on the site of a villa owned by benefactor Harold Guylee Chester (1887-1973). It is the Methodist youth centre and provides accommodation.

Above: William Grimshaw opened in 1955 in Creighton Avenue as a secondary modern school, named after a former Hornsey mayor. In 1967 it became the north wing of Creighton comprehensive, the south wing being a 1955 block built for the amalgamated Tollington boys and girls schools. It is now called Fortismere.

This temporary public garden in Fortis Green Road was one of several post-war bomb sites which Hornsey councillor Frederick Cleary successfully campaigned to be 'beautified'. It was on the corner with Princes Avenue, opposite the existing corner garden.

In 1959 the bomb-site garden disappeared to be replaced by the pub The John Baird. No pubs were built by the Edwardian developers of Muswell Hill because of opposition by the temperance movement and this was the first new one. It was named after the television pioneer who worked at Alexandra Palace.

By 1963 when this photograph was taken, the Royal Oak in St James's Lane had become dilapidated. Its sign board at the top had gone and a lean-to added.

The old pub, which was extremely small inside, was demolished and by 1966 had been replaced. The design of the new Royal Oak imitates the weatherboard exterior of the former building.

Pre-war work to electrify the branch line to the Palace, nearly completed, was abandoned by London Transport. Steam trains continued to provide a passenger service until July 1954, as shown in this view of Cranley Gardens station.

A porter signals the departure of one of the last trains at Cranley Gardens station which had opened in 1902. Goods trains continued to use the line for a few years but the rails were taken up in 1971.

This 1960 photograph, with Woodside Avenue on the right, shows how the line had overgrown. The land was acquired in stages by Haringey Council and officially opened in 1984 as the Parkland Walk, a four-and-a-half mile linear green walkway. It is now a statutory local nature reserve.

In November 1959 the railway bridge at the top of Muswell Hill was widened, no doubt a reflection of the way road traffic was increasing. The most noticeable changes in the appearance of Muswell Hill from Edwardian times onwards are those due to the impact of an increased volume of road vehicles.

Another example is Colney Hatch Lane which was regarded as too narrow in the stretch north of Pages Lane. In 1960 it was widened with the loss of these mature trees. Road markings had not yet been laid down here.

The barrenness of Colney Hatch Lane in 1961 after the trees had gone is shown by this photograph. Steam rollers work on a new road surface and temporary road markings were introduced. Newly built Essex Lodge (left) replaced a Regency villa.

Muswell Hill in January 1962 with snow proving a hazard for drivers. The accident seems to have occurred at the junction of the hill with Cascade Avenue.

Newly built Craven Terrace, Nos 12-24 Muswell Hill, photographed in 1960 when the seven 'contemporary' houses were up for sale by estate agents Normans. Standing above Grosvenor Gardens and below Springfield Avenue they occupy a bomb site and are set well back on Muswell Hill.

After passenger and then goods traffic ceased on the branch line to the Palace, Muswell Hill railway station was demolished. A garden area was provided in its place, constructed by 1960 when this photograph was taken. Risborough Close is opposite (left).

The Athenaeum in 1963, three years before its demolition and replacement by a block of flats with a Sainsbury supermarket at ground level. Cinemas and halls were targeted in the 1960s as large sites for the new supermarkets were being sought. The Odeon opposite the Athenaeum also had a car park at the rear and although threatened managed to escape demolition.

A synagogue was built in 1965 in Tetherdown following the loss of space used for worship in the Athenaeum. The building on the west side of Tetherdown is by architect Joe Mendleson.

On 6 November 1965 Cllr Vic Butler, Mayor of Haringey, opened a new medical clinic in Fortis Green. It had been built on the site of the former fire station. The firemen's cottages remained behind. Haringey had replaced Hornsey as the local authority in 1965.

This block of flats had been built in Fortis Green by 1958. They stood nearly opposite the police station and were provided in order to house police officers. Appropriately they were named The Copse. The flats are now in private ownership.

In January 1960 the postal address of Muswell Hill Broadway was created replacing Queens Parade, Muswell Hill Road' and similar parade addresses. The southern part of Colney Hatch Lane became Muswell Hill Broadway as shown in the road sign outside the post office in this 1963 photograph. The facade of the post office had been rebuilt in 1936; the date stone with GVR cypher has subsequently been covered over by signage.

In 1963 Woolworth's store was enlarged. The company had traded in Muswell Hill since the 1930s. For many years a flower seller traded regularly here.

Some traditional shop blinds, once widespread, are still to be seen in this 1963 photograph of the shops between Woolworth and the roundabout. Radio Rentals benefited from the television boom that took place in the 1960s. Tesco was to transform itself with giant supermarkets provided with car parks, though no parked cars are seen in this view.

The sign outside Northern House in the Exchange parade of shops says 'Closing Down'. This large department store, with entrances at both No. 13 and No. 16 was a good supplier of drapery items. Previously the shop had been Summersby and before that Nicholsons. It still traded in 1958 but did not survive the 1960s.

This 1963 photograph shows the Singer shop opposite the Odeon which recently has traded under another name. Modish 1950s flowerbeds adorn the pavement corners.

Grand Parade, Portis Green Road in 1963. There is still plenty of space to park a car. The increase in traffic, decade by decade, has done much to change the scene.

Left: The Congregational church on the corner of Tetherdown and Queens Avenue dated from 1897 and was a built on a site donated by Edmondson. In this April 1964 photograph it is without a porch.

Below: The Congregationalists combined with the Presbyterians in 1972 to form a United Reformed church. The Presbyterians gave up their Broadway church which is now a pub. A porch was added to this building. The Belisha beacon crossing gave way to traffic lights.

six

Recent
Decades

Delicatessen shops selling delicacies or relishes for the table probably originated in the nineteenth century in the United States. This one was photographed in 1978 in Fortis Green Road, with the proprietor, Mr R.W. Flack, seen through the window.

Fishmongers selling fresh fish have been welcome traders in Muswell Hill. This is J.B. Green's shop at No. 52 Broadway in 1978. By 2006, still operating, it had become Walter Purkis & Sons. The branch of MacFisheries across the road at No. 111 Broadway did not survive.

Pulham & Sons, butchers, traded most of the twentieth century at this shop, once No. 16 Victoria Parade and then No. 26 Muswell Hill Broadway. It also traded at No. 161 and No. 440 Broadway and other butchers were Dewhurst (at No. 300), Gunner (at No. 233) and West (at No. 123). Supermarket competition swept them away.

Fruit and vegetable shops seem to survive better than butchers though this one has gone, its space taken by Crocodile Antiques. Bond & White, builders merchants lost their brick-built building (left) in 1970 and it became a supermarket, first Budgens then Marks & Spencer who took over the two shops built on the front of the pair of Victorian villas.

Leonard Lyle, men's outfitters, in January 1980. They traded at Nos 25-27 Muswell Hill Broadway, near Fortis Green Road, and the shops are now occupied by Ryman and Moss Bros.

Queens Parade, built in 1897, now Nos 97–211 Muswell Hill Broadway, is the heart of Muswell Hill. Although the occupiers of the shops over 110 years have constantly changed (with Martyns a notable exception) shops are rarely empty and unused.

Some shops continue to sell the same produce even though the owners change. The shop on the corner of Princes Avenue and the Broadway has always been a wine merchants. Jeans are a later cultural arrival. The daily bustle of the Broadway is captured in this 1970s photograph.

Langston's clock, installed in Edwardian times above what is now No. 71 Muswell Hill Broadway, is still in place. It does not work and the shop is no longer a jeweller but a ladies' clothes shop. The St James's church clock dating from the 1840s and recently repaired, is still a handy guide to the time.

The southern end of Colney Hatch Lane, now the Broadway, is also popular for shopping. The National Wine Stores was taken over by adjacent Barclays Bank but a retail presence maintained on the street by The Jewellery Exchange, a popular antiques shop run by Andrew Rowan at No. 225. Shoe shop H. Levison went and is now empty.

The Children's Bookshop at No. 29 Portis Green Road, formerly Firs Parade, was established there in 1974. Its success as a well-stocked shop has brought it awards. Andreas, also in this 1981 photograph, still trades there too. The estate agency was established in Edwardian times as the estate office for W.J. Collins.

The John Baird pub seems to have become a good social centre in this 1978 photograph of the interior. The well-dressed customers, one smoking a pipe, seem to be retired people.

Muswell Hill Broadway is at the edge of a small plateau with the land falling steeply to the south-east, with some of the sloping land used as a car park, though in Edwardian times it was a pleasure garden with a theatre-cum-cinema called Summerlands. This Marks & Spencer extension is one of Muswell Hill's new buildings, overlooking the car park.

Muswell Hill's most spectacular view is from Hillfield Park's top end, with London spread out below. The properties here, built by Edmondson over the former Hillfield estate, seem to tumble down the hill, capacious and full of windows.

Especially prominent because of its location is the tower and spire of St James's church, which can be seen easily from distant places and gives Muswell Hill much of it character. The suburb's geographical setting makes it distinctive.

The Salvation Army's brass band gathers outside Barclay's Bank, with the library seen in the background. Stirring occasions like this do not often happen in Muswell Hill. This was probably in December in the lead up to Christmas.

On 10 July 1980 Alexandra Palace caught fire in the afternoon, the wind blowing the flames towards the west side of the building. The Great Hall was devastated as well as the Palm Court. In 1983 a planning enquiry ruling allowed the trustees to develop it for exhibitions and it was resolved to rebuild it using insurance money.

As a first step a temporary Alexandra Pavilion was commissioned for a site on the east side seen in the background in this photograph. Used for exhibitions, the building stood there until 1990. Its location is now a car park.

This fountain is in a small garden on the east side of the Palace. It dates from 1875 when it stood in the Italian Garden, a courtyard within the building. During reconstruction this area became a new West Hall and the fountain was moved outside.

During the rebuilding of the Palace, which reopened in 1988, local people successfully campaigned for the derelict railway station on the north side of the Palace to be converted into a community centre. It is known as CUFOS – Community Use for the Old Station.

In July 1984 George Thomas, Viscount Tonypandy, former Speaker of the House of Commons and former vice-president of the Methodist Conference, laid the foundation stone for a new church attached to North Bank. Designed by architects Knollt & Lelliot, it replaced the Colney Hatch Lane building which suffered cracking.

Springfield House, also in Pages Lane, dates back to the 1860s. For most of the twentieth century it was occupied by nuns as a convent with a school building added onto it. In 2001 it was converted into three residential properties and renamed St Martin's Terrace.

A tall brick-built office block replaced the ABC cinema at the top of Muswell Hill from 1980. Its design and materials were influenced by advice from the Muswell Hill Conservation Area Advisory Committee. Muswell Hill had been made a conservation area under late 1970s legislation which provided for them. Local volunteers, including architects, vet planning applications.

William Brannan Collins, son of the developer W.J. Collins, was responsible for the design of many of the domestic properties on the Rookfield Garden Village estate. Local residents mounted this plaque to his memory in Rookfield Close.

Left: No. 11 The Exchange was occupied by the National Provincial Bank. In 1962 this banking company was taken over by the Westminster Bank which in 1970 renamed itself NatWest. This 1950s view shows the bank still as the National Provincial.

Below: In 1927 the Westminster Bank had opened nearby in the Summerlands Mansions block close to where Lloyds Bank had just built its branch on the corner of Summerland Gardens. NatWest maintained both branches until the 1990s when the former National Provincial premises were closed and its NatWest sign removed. This 1995 photograph shows the empty building, soon to become a restaurant.

Above: Eating out became popular and more restaurants took over Muswell Hill's retail outlets. Toffs was one of the first, established in 1968 by the Toffali family and now run by the Georgiou brothers. It has won prizes as 'fish and chip shop of the year' and other awards.

Below: Changes in church attendances meant that in 2001 this sale board notice went up outside the former United Reformed church premises in Alexandra Park Road. Built in 1907 in fine period style by architects Mummery & Fleming-Williams, it catered for worshippers at the Whitfields Tabernacle in Finsbury who had moved to the new suburb. It has been converted into apartments.

In 1976 the Muswell Hill Festival began, located at first in the car park off Summerland Gardens, then in The Grove. This July 1995 event was held in Fortis Green Road one Sunday when traffic was diverted. A music stage was erected outside the Odeon.

Local societies took stalls and artists and craft people displayed their work. Events took place in St James's Hall and in the corner park. Proceeds went to the Hornsey Trust for children with cerebral palsy. The festival has moved to a larger site in Cherry Tree Wood.

This Abbey National branch in the former Exchange, photographed in 1995 moved the following year into larger premises at Nos 105-11 Muswell Hill Broadway. The premises became Falconer's art shop and a large plate glass window was installed.

Falconers left in 2004 and new owner Chris Oswald gave the window (now cracked) a new look inspired by Spanish architect Antonio Gaudi. Its design split the community. A government planning inspector ruled that it must be replaced.

Left: Alexandra Palace rebuilt in 1875 after the 1873 fire and rebuilt again by 1988 after the 1980 fire, continues to survive, attracting visitors for ice-skating, exhibitions, conferences, pop concerts, firework displays and sometimes an organ recital. Leased to a private developer in 2006, its future role is awaited.

Below: The White House has stood at the top of Muswell Hill from at least the eighteenth century. For much of the twentieth century it was occupied by estate agents. In its latest manifestation it is an internet café, a sign of the times, and one more addition to the history of Muswell Hill.

Index

Other local titles published by Tempus

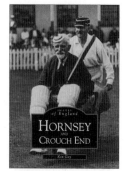

Hornsey and Crouch End
KEN GAY

The changes in the villages of Hornsey and Crouch End are depicted mainly through the archives of the Hornsey Historical Society, of which Ken Gay is an active member. Some views show the last days of the rural scene; others show the new houses and public buildings as well as the people who, by the Edwardian era, were part of the growing population of the Borough of Hornsey.

0 7524 1072 5

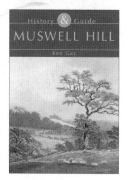

Muswell Hill: History and Guide
KEN GAY

Not urbanised until the end of the nineteenth century, Muswell Hill was quickly built up as a middle-class suburb with shopping parades, domestic houses set in tree-lined avenues and many churches. In this volume, Ken Gay uses over 150 views to illuminate Muswell Hill's unfolding story. In addition a guided tour introduces routes by which the suburbs past and present can be explored.

0 7524 2604 4

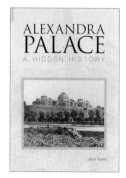

Alexandra Palace: A Hidden History
JANET HARRIS

This book chronicles the hidden history of Alexandra Palace and details the episode in the Palace's history when it became home to thousands of German civilian internees during and after the First World War. Using images from the Bruce Castle Museum's extensive picture archives and personal recollections from those who were interned here and their families, *Alexandra Palace* sheds light on a little known history of this most famous landmark.

0 7524 3636 8

City of Westminster
BRIAN GIRLING

With over 200 old images, *City of Westminster* leads the reader around Pimlico, through Belgravia and Knightsbridge, Mayfair and St James' and on to Soho and the West End's famous theatreland. There are pictures of vanished neighbourhoods, street characters, busy markets, trams, horse-drawn buses and old theatres. We see the Thames frozen, the Dorchester Hotel being built, Suffragettes in Knightsbridge and an Edwardian driving school in Soho.

0 7524 3191 9

If you are interested in purchasing other books published by Tempus, or in case you have difficulty finding any Tempus books in your local bookshop, you can also place orders directly through our website
www.tempus-publishing.com